think  hear  see

g k hepp

I THINK I HEAR I SEE

published by IPBooks, Queens, NY

Copyright © 2024
g k hepp

ISBN: 978-1-956864-79-3

A
celebration
of
collaboration

"iPhone as iBook"

Teatro Municipale Valli
Reggio Emilia, 2007

The Orchestra Mozart was founded in 2004 to afford talented young musicians the opportunity to play in a world-class orchestra, with world-class conductors.

Bach: Brandenburg Concerto No. 5 | Claudio Abbado & the Orchestra Mozart

https://youtu.be/gIgqeA76cdU?si=qUcDbb4BHgIChZ1o

What is also special about the Fifth Brandenburg Concerto is that Bach gave the harpsichord a prominent role. In the first movement, this tradition-steeped keyboard instrument has a three-minute solo passage that is brilliantly handled by Ottavio Dantone (05:56). Because of this harpsichord solo, the Brandenburg Concerto No. 5 is considered perhaps the earliest example of a solo concerto for a keyboard instrument.

Dantone plays a harpsichord from the workshop of William Horn, which is also a feast for the eyes with its many decorations on a bright red base in the middle of the stage. The Latin quotation in the lid of the ornate keyboard instrument 'Nulla scientia melior musica animae harmonia' (There is no science better than the music of the soul) could have been written just for this Brandenburg Concerto, which seems to have drawn its rhythm from the pulse of the human soul.

turtles

all

the

way
down

cosmogony

intelligent design
needs a designer
but who designed the designer
it is turtles all the way down

enigmas

...in the beginning
there was noise

then creation
in silence

by design
perhaps...

the world starts with
a big bang
something from nothing
what was before
how can it be
will it end in a whimper
or was there an intelegent
designer
who had a plan
for beast and man
for you and me
divinity

Subject: **What is the IQ of AI ?**

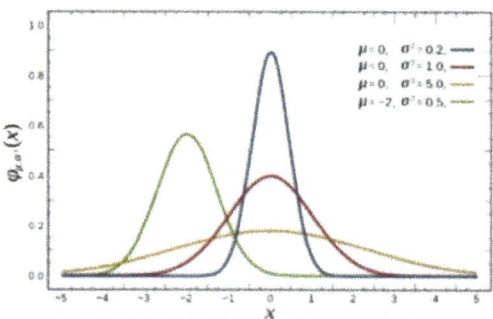

A selection of Normal Distribution
Probability Density Functions (PDFs).
Both the mean, μ, and variance, σ², are
varied. The key is given on the graph.

Born: June 28, 1971 (age 52 years), Pretoria, South Africa

No Person except a natural born Citizen, or a Citizen of the United States, at the time of the Adoption of this Constitution, shall be eligible to the Office of President; neither shall any Person be eligible to that Office who shall not have attained to the Age of thirty five Years, and been fourteen Years a Resident ...

CERTIFICATE OF LIVE BIRTH

The Order of Things

1966 book by French philosopher Michel Foucault

Epistemic interpretation

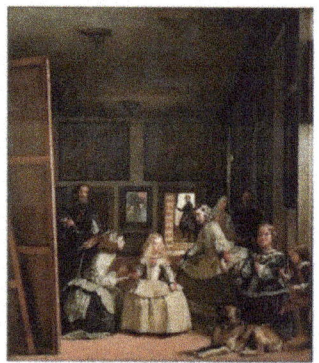

Las Meninas (*The Ladies-in-waiting*, 1656), by Diego Velázquez. (Museo

The Order of Things (1966) is about the "cognitive status of the modern human sciences" in the production of knowledge — the ways of seeing that researchers apply to a subject

We are looking at a picture in which the painter is, in turn, looking out at us. A mere confrontation, eyes catching one another's glance, direct looks superimposing themselves upon one another as they cross.

And yet, this slender line of reciprocal visibility embraces a whole complex network of uncertainties, exchanges, and feints. The painter is turning his eyes towards us only in so far as we happen to occupy the same position as his subject.[7][8]

Why Cranes?

Cranes form an ancient group, the earliest fossils having been recovered from Eocene deposits in North America. Living forms are found worldwide except in South America, but populations of many are endangered by hunting and habitat destruction.

Endangered!

Like humans, flamingos make friends for life

A group of flamingoes is called a "flamboyance".[2]

Matthew Bourne's Ballet Clips- "Swan Lake"

The Art of Dance is a discipline, yet it is still ever changing and expanding. Art in and of itself is meant to provoke thought, discourse, open minds and hearts to the possibility of more than the reality one currently lives in, to challenge thought and promote change in society.

Alice trying to play croquet with a
Flamingo

face the music

Cadenza

Improvised solo between
musical sections

**Karl Richter - Brandenburg
Concerto 5 (harpsichord
solo)**

https://youtu.be/vMSwVf_69Hc?
si=V_kfudHQUC_K6O7Y

Ounce Gold Donald Trump Round

———

Commonwealth Club

———

Victory47 Cologne by President Trump | $99

Definition

1 : one that sneaks

The MAGA Bible : Handmade

30-day returns

suggests he read
verse on adultery

~~~~~~~~~~~~~~~~~~~~~~~~~~~~

4" Mr President Donald Trump Rubber Duck 2024
Electoion with USA Flag MAGA Squeak Bath Toys Stars and
Stripes American Patriotic Rubber Duckies Decoration
Baby Adults, Yellow

peek-a-boo ❗

Life of Her Party

watershed

Biden falters in high-stakes debate, Trump spews falsehoods

Harris Walz

'Bringing back the joy': Walz's first day

MAGA   RINO

**Royal Fairytale Tour
Neuschwanstein,**

Magic Kingdom

♪♪

Chartres Cathedral

Sagrada Familia

Old Faithful

HATTUSA WAS ORIGINALLY FOUNDED BY THE HATTI IN 2500 BCE,

This very important complex and those who built it along with their vast empire, however, remained almost unknown until their writings were discovered, first by the Irish missionary William Wright in 1884

"good food good mood"

Persian manuscript Nimatnama-i-Nasiruddin-Shahi explaining how samosas should be cooked

$$$

Pachira Braid, Money
Tree in 6 in. Grower Pot

The jade screen was directly in front of
Freud as he worked and consulted with
patients and Clunas believes it represented
all that Freud felt his theories could not
explain. At that time the shadowy world of
an imagined "Orient" to the east was widely
set in contrast to the western tradition of
logical thought and classical culture.

violence

mourning has broken
10/7/23

afterlives
live in lyrics
embedded
in songs
enstoned

PALESTINIAN CIVILIANS EVACUATE FROM RAFAH

'Blue Screen of Death'

A faulty **software update** by **CrowdStrike**, an American **cybersecurity** company, causes **global computer outages**.

The Start of the Race of the Riderless Horses

1820

Horace Vernet French

"A dark horse riderless, bolts like a phantom past the winning post, his mane moonflowing, his eyeballs stars."

— James Joyce

Current status of abortion access across the United States

Banned ◼ Legal with gestational limit of 6-18 weeks ◼ Legal

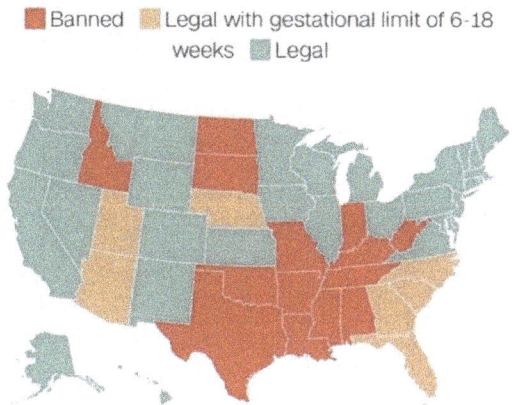

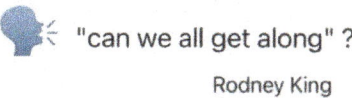 "can we all get along" ?

Rodney King

Who voted majority for Dobbs v Jackson?

Justice Samuel Alito delivered the court's majority opinion. Justices Clarence Thomas and Brett Kavanaugh filed concurring opinions, and Chief Justice John Roberts filed an opinion concurring in the judgment. Justices Stephen Breyer, Sonia Sotomayor, and Elena Kagan filed a dissenting opinion.

🗣️ "You could have recused yourself"

Quote for today

"The Supreme Court is now the most dangerous branch of our government" Laurence Tribe NYRB

supremest
presumest

four score
and ten
years ago
the people
of Weimar
elected
one
among them
to lead them
into
an abyss

the
"third"

what
were
the
first
and
second ?

-

what
were
the
second
and
first ?

does anyone remember

rehearsals...

practice for a fourth ?

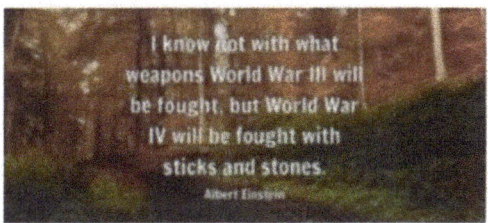

I know not with what
weapons World War III will
be fought, but World War
IV will be fought with
sticks and stones.

Albert Einstein

what if
another
had been chosen ?

Subject: **Fantasy**

Subject: Reality

During World War II, the Germans
used the Enigma, a cipher machine,
to develop nearly unbreakable
codes for sending secret messages.
The Enigma's settings offered
150,000,000,000,000,000,000
possible solutions, yet the Allies
were eventually able to crack its
code.

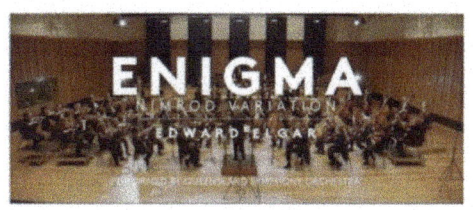

**Edward Elgar - Enigma Variations
Op.36: IX. (Nimrod)**

https://youtu.be/7iM5dymBBl4?
si=Fj1Cv5ziZxCMoLJJ

In 1899, English composer Edward Elgar
created his Enigma Variations; a set of
variations on the one melody, with each
one representing a different friend of his.
From his wife to his music publisher,
each friend was immortalised in music
as their different personalities shone
through. This piece has never lost
popularity, especially with the moving
and powerful 'Nimrod' variation.

Flemish Proverbs

In a dream, I was meeting with a rabbi in an alcove in a painting by Pieter Bruegel. Upon awakening, I was relieved it had not been a painting by Hieronymus Bosch.

Ship of Fools

Pieter Bruegel's *The Tower of Babel* depicts a traditional Nimrod inspecting stonemasons.

Some say the story of the Tower of Babel can help answer modern questions, such as the physical differences between people groups and language changes.

Generative AI is experimental.

"mensch"
in French
"personne"
means
"person"
and
"no one"
in English

culled from google
assembled by me

trans

gen

er

a

tion

al

i

t

partimento

So, what is a partimento? A good definition is a metaphor: **a partimento is a thread that contains in itself all, or most, of the information needed for a complete composition... The partimento ... is a linear entity that runs from the beginning to the end of a (potential)**

composition.[4]

Your login attempt failed. Your password must include a capital letter, a lowercase letter, a number and a special character.

Your login attempt failed. Your password must include a letter, a number and a Chinese character.

"cinq à sept" on a parapet

Google it

Portrait of an Artist as a Young Pup

"🙂rise 🙂set"

wake up
Lily is up
stretching
kissing kissing
shake shake shake!

how does she shake like that?
humans cannot do that like that

"dog is god spelled backwards"

"cognito ergo sum"

something to think about
every morning

her beady eyes
stare at mine
closed
pretending to be asleep
she moves her nose to mine
to see if I am breathing
if I am awake

I open my eyes
our day begins

long ago
I was loved
and loved
as Lily loves
and is loved

before worlds
of words

where music speaks
to a universe
that sings
a language
that speaks itself

where meaning
is as it sounds
Creation
itself

awe
sweet light
and wrath
wrath of an imagined God

before
lives in The Garden
knew not what they did

ergo
non cognito

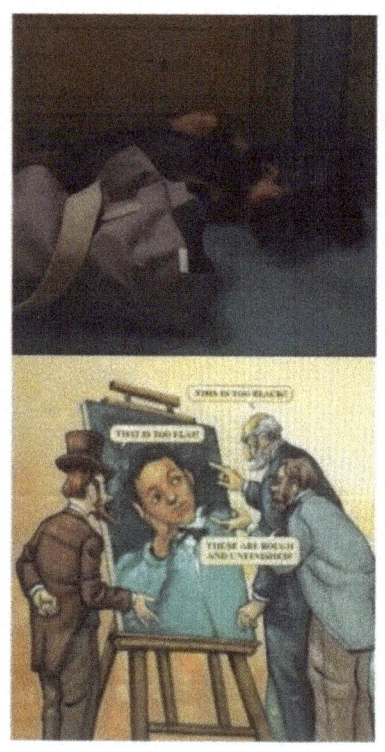

"Every artist dips his brush into his own soul and paints his nature into his pictures"

https://youtu.be/RzEEVkZUbS8?si=VIdVXhuJLvPn4Nxx

EMBEDDED LANGUAGE

◆ ...the fourth the fifth
(test levels, there were eight)

◆ ...the minor fall

◆ ...the major lift

◆ ...faith was strong

◆ ...overthrew you
(overhead throw triple twist)

◆ ...tied to a kitchen chair
(spin with foot connection)

◆ ...cut your hair
(spin, her blade to her hair)

◆ ...did my best

◆ ...all went wrong
(always a possibility)

◆ FINAL SPIN
(forward inside death spiral)

◆ ...I'll stand before the lords of song
(JUDGES)

◆ ...with nothing on my tongue but
"HALLELUJA" ‼

face à face

tête-à-tête chair

know thyself
warned Socrates
who knew
to know
himself

ask your self
objective self
to ask
yourself
who am I

?

in time
you will know
who you were
before you became
who you are

"It is astonishing that one awakes and is already oneself,"

first
"Do no harm"

be kind
of the kind that asks
"What is the decent thing to do"?

keep
yourself to yourself

hide
from yourself

protect
yourself

ask yourself
"...what do I know how to do"?

do it!

prepare
yourself

"Are you ready"?

some say
"People crave mediocrity"

Father says
"Who knows knows"
"Who doesn't know is the boss"

Mother says
"now I've heard everything"!

"What did the Critics say"?

"It's nice that your Mother liked it"!!

"...so it goes"
Kurt Vonnegut is said to have said

▲ ▼ Les Rousseaus

Henri Rousseau: Myself: Portrait-Landscape

 66 Man is born free, but is everywhere in chains.

Jean-Jacques Rousseau. The Social Contract

...**"but what do I know"**

 66 The greatest thing in the world is to
know how to belong to oneself.

Michel de Montaigne, The Complete
Essays
Tags: ataraxy, independence,
individuality, inspirational, self-
assurance, self-awareness, self-
containment, self-determination, self-
esteem, self-reliance, self-respect, self-
sufficiency, self-trust, solitude

ataraxia

: calmness untroubled by
mental or emotional disquiet

your business
my business
mind your own business

🗣 "business"
like snow
spread
to
infinity

⛄ melted

agreed

becomes
"divinity" *

*

    : fudge made of whipped egg
    whites, sugar, and nuts

How to Observe the Northern Lights This Weekend

The Space Weather Prediction Center said solar activity would be high again on Saturday.

May 10, 2024

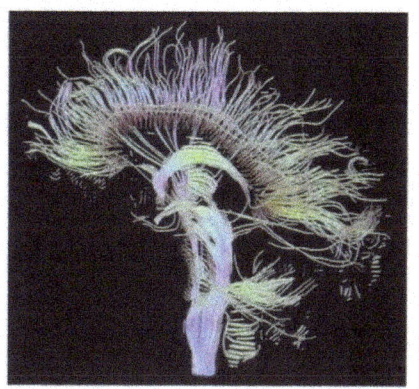

An image of neural pathways in the brain taken using diffusion tensor imaging

Sent from my iPhone

Solar eclipse of April 8, 2024/Location